WELLHOUSE PLAN VIEW

CROWN OF SHADOWS

LOCKE & KEY

VOLUME 3

WRITTEN BY

JOE HILL

ART BY

GABRIEL RODRIGUEZ

Written by: Joe Hill

Art by: Gabriel Rodriguez

Colors by: Jay Fotos

Letters by: Robbie Robbins

Series Edited by: Chris Ryall

Collection Edited by: Justin Eisinger

Collection Designed by: Robbie Robbins

Locke & Key created by Joe Hill and Gabriel Rodriguez

ISBN: 978-1-60010-695-8   18 17 16 15   7 8 9 10

IDW®

Ted Adams, CEO & Publisher
Greg Goldstein, Chief Operating Officer
Robbie Robbins, EVP/Sr. Graphic Artist
Chris Ryall, Chief Creative Officer/Editor-in-Chief
Matthew Ruzicka, CPA, Chief Financial Officer
Alan Payne, VP of Sales

Become our fan on Facebook **facebook.com/idwpublishing**
Follow us on Twitter **@idwpublishing**
Check us out on YouTube **youtube.com/idwpublishing**
www.IDWPUBLISHING.com

introduction by Brian K. Vaughan

Wait, you're just reading Crown of Shadows *now*?

What the hell took you so long?

Look, I fully understand the appeal of "waiting for the trade," and IDW puts together some lovely compilations, but *Locke & Key* is one of the few ongoing comics that demands to be read the day a new issue is released. Since the first page of the first installment, it's been a top-of-the-pile series for me every single month it's come out.

(Incidentally, way back when I still had hair, I used to put my favorite comics from that week's purchases on the *bottom* of my to-read pile, as a little reward for making it through whatever crap I was just buying out of habit. But now that I'm busy and old, I try to read the good stuff the second it's in my hands, and the crap never.)

Anyway, if you've already read the first two storylines of this epic-in-the-making, you know it's not good, it's fucking great. There's just not another book on the stands quite like this, is there? The mythology of the world is vast and imaginative, but the family at its core is so real, so relatable.

Like I said, I can never wait for these collections, so I don't know if any of my fellow introducers have already made this obvious connection, but Joe Hill and Gabriel Rodriguez fit together as elegantly as their title. Unlike most of us lowly funny-book writers, Joe is a first-rate novelist who doesn't need an artist to make him look good. And any silent panel in this collection is proof enough that Gabriel doesn't need a bunch of highfalutin words to tell a story beautifully. But man, together, these guys sing. I'm pretty sure this is their first collaboration, and already the bastards harmonize as well as seasoned duos like Gaiman & McKean, Morrison & Quitely, and Ennis & Dillon.

I mean, just look at how perfectly each scene is paced, how thoughtfully every single page is constructed. I once told another writer that while comics can be creepy or unsettling, they're almost never frightening. Without the benefit of music, sound design, and editing, I think it's tough for most fiction to elicit genuine fear. But I'll be damned if there aren't a few moments in this arc (particularly during the haunting stand-alone coda) that rank right up there with some of the scariest scenes from those early Moore/Bissette/Totleben issues of *Swamp Thing*.

And while the supernatural stuff is brilliant (I will never tire of learning about new keys), the reason I'm afraid is because of how much I've come to care about Tyler, Kinsey, and especially Bode. Those kids aren't characters, they're people.

Readers love fantasy, but we *need* horror. Smart horror. Truthful horror. Horror that helps us make sense of a cruelly senseless world. *Locke & Key* is all of those things... and somehow, every so often, it's also really goddamn funny. Now that's just showing off.

Whatever, we've wasted too much time already. What the hell are you waiting for? Come on in.

Door's open.

14

"CLOSETS AND CAVES, SINKS AND CISTERNS.

"ANYTHING BIG AND HOLLOW.

"CANYONS AND DRAINAGE PIPES. BASEMENTS AND ATTICS.

"AND YOU, SAM. YOUR SOUL WAS ONE ENORMOUS EMPTY SPACE.

HELP ME

"YOU WERE A CUP WITH NOTHING IN IT UNTIL I CAME ALONG TO FILL YOU UP. YOU WERE JUST WHAT I NEEDED. I COULD SPEAK TO YOU ANYWHERE, ANYTIME."

I NEEDED HELP.

AND I GAVE IT TO YOU.

YOU TOOK WHAT YOU WANTED FROM ME AND THEN THREW ME AWAY. LITERALLY LEFT ME FOR DEAD.

NOW YOU'RE HERE BECAUSE YOU THINK YOU CAN GET SOMETHING MORE FROM ME. AND PEOPLE THOUGHT I WAS DELUDED.

I'M HERE BECAUSE I'M YOUR FRIEND. THE ONLY ONE YOU HAVE. BELIEVE ME, SAM. I DON'T NEED YOU.

IF YOU WON'T HELP ME, THERE ARE OTHER WAYS TO FIND THE KEY TO THE BLACK DOOR.

YOU SURE WE CAN'T MAKE A DEAL? I JUST WANT YOU TO BE HAPPY, SAM. WHAT WOULD MAKE YOU HAPPY?

TO HAVE NEVER LIVED AT ALL. TO BE WIPED FROM THE WORLD, TO BE DESTROYED COMPLETELY, AND TO TAKE YOU WITH ME.

MY HAND ON YOUR THROAT, ALL THE WAY TO OBLIVION. YOU DESTROYED ME. NOTHING WOULD MAKE ME HAPPIER THAN RETURNING THE FAVOR.

KRESSH!

THE HELL?

IT HURTS.

IT FEELS SO GOOD.

IS SOMEONE IN THERE? KINSEY? BODE?

HELLO?

Crown Of
Shadows

CHAPTER TWO:
IN THE CAVE

COL. ADAM CRAIS
MAY 18 ~ JUNE 4
1736 1780

«The Dreams and Ideas
of Free Men are as an
Army of Shadows, and
as impossible to
strike down...»

HEY,
JORDAN. HOW
ARE YOU?

FUCKED.
COMPLETELY
FUCKED.

OH. I'M—
SORRY TO
HEAR IT. CAN
I SIT WITH
YOU?

YES.

FINISH THE
PAPER FOR
ETHICS?

NO.

DOWNLOADED A
PAPER ON THE TOPIC.
BUT I'M NOT GOING TO
TURN IT IN. I THINK IF YOU
CHEAT IN AN ETHICS
CLASS THEN THERE'S
REALLY NO HOPE
FOR YOU.

MAYBE *I* FANCY *HIM.*

I DON'T SEE IT, MYSELF. NOT BASED ON WHAT I KNOW ABOUT YOU.

WHAT YOU— EXCUSE ME, BUT WHAT DO YOU IMAGINE YOU KNOW ABOUT ME? WHO *ARE* YOU?

SCOT KAVANAUGH. YOU STUCK YOUR HEAD OUT A WINDOW AND NEARLY THREW UP ON ME A FEW WEEKS AGO, BUT OTHER THAN THAT, WE'VE HAD LITTLE CONTACT.

OH. SORRY.

AT THE TIME YOU WERE DRESSING LIKE THE GIRLS IN THE TEAM SPIRIT CLUB AND WEARING YOUR HAIR LIKE SOMEONE IN A YOUNG CHRISTIAN PRAYER GROUP.

I'D HAVE THROWN UP, TOO. NATURAL RESPONSE TO SWALLOWING A TOXIC SUBSTANCE.

WHAT TOXIC SUBSTANCE?

ABERCROMBIE & FITCH PREP SCHOOL BANALITY. YOU DON'T REALLY FANCY THE DARK-HARIED BOY, DO YOU?

I DO. HE'S COOL.

NOTHING BUT. THAT'S HIS PROBLEM. I LIKE HIS ALTERNATIVE BUT NOT-TOO-ALTERNATIVE LIP RING. THAT WAY HE CAN BE EDGY BUT STILL SNEER AT ANYONE WHO'S REALLY DIFFERENT.

HE DOESN'T SNEER AT PEOPLE. HE'S A NICE GUY.

YOU DON'T KNOW ONE THING ABOUT HIM. OR ABOUT ME.

OH NO. THERE IS *ONE* THING I KNOW ABOUT YOU.

BOY, I CAN HARDLY WAIT. ACTUALLY, I REALLY *CAN'T* WAIT. I'M MEETING A FRIEND IN THE LIBRARY.

I KNOW YOUR FATHER'S NAME WAS RENDELL LOCKE.

SO WHAT?

AND IT HAPPENS HIS NAME IS WRITTEN ON A WALL IN THE DROWNING CAVE. ALONG WITH SOME OTHER STUFF. EVER BEEN THERE?

WHAT'S THIS CAVE?

KIDS FROM THIS SCHOOL HAVE BEEN GOING THERE FOR YEARS TO DRINK AND MAKE OUT.

BUT NO ONE HAS EVER GONE DEEPER INTO THEM THAN ME. NOT COUNTING THE KIDS WHO DIED.

WHAT KIDS?

I'M NOT TOO CLEAR ON THAT REALLY. SOME UNLUCKY BLOKES IN THE '70S OR SOMETHING WENT DOWN THERE TO GET STONED AND DROWNED WHEN THE TIDE CAME IN.

YOU SEE, THE LOWER LEVELS ARE ALL FLOODED OUT, AND THE WATER IS KNOWN TO SUDDENLY RISE AT HIGH TIDE.

SHOW ME.

LOVE TO. THIS AFTERNOON. AFTER LAST BELL.

OH, AND I WANT SOMETHING IN RETURN, FOR LEADING YOU TO THE PLACE WHERE YOUR FATHER PUT HIS MARK.

I WANT TO ASK YOU THREE QUESTIONS, WHICH YOU HAVE TO ANSWER TRUTHFULLY.

WHY?

I FIGURED I WAS MORE LIKELY TO GET THAT THAN A MAKE-OUT SESSION.

WELL. YOU CALLED THAT ONE RIGHT.

WHICH IS SILLY, HONESTLY. THE TRUTH IS ALWAYS MORE SCARY THAN KISSING SOMEONE FOR THE FIRST TIME.

NOW I WARN YOU, IT'S QUITE DARK DOWN THERE IN THE CAVE.

I'M NOT SCARED OF THE DARK AND I'M NOT SCARED OF KISSING AND I'M SURE AS HELL NOT SCARED OF THE TRUTH. I'LL SEE YOU BACK HERE AFTER LAST BELL.

BRILLIANT.

HOW'D I DO?

THE WAVES OF LOATHING COMING OFF HER WERE DEFINITELY LESS INTENSE BY THE TIME SHE WALKED AWAY.

BESIDES. YOU KNOW WHAT WE WERE TALKING ABOUT IN PSYCH YESTERDAY? THERE'S THIS WHOLE THEORY THAT A LOT OF TIMES DISGUST HIDES SECRET, INTENSE DESIRE.

AND YOU THINK THIS IS THE CASE HERE?

NAH. NOT REALLY. JUST TRYING TO CHEER YOU UP.

THE WATER. THE CHRISTING WATER.

WHAT ARE YOU SAYING? THERE DIDN'T USED TO BE WATER HERE?

NOT SO MUCH. IT WAS LOWER. MUST CHANGE WITH THE TIDES. LAST TIME WE CAME OUT HERE, IT HAD TO BE SIX FEET LOWER AT LEAST.

I KNEW THIS WAS BULLSHIT.

THE HELL IT IS. HIS NAME WAS WRITTEN ON THE WALL, MAYBE TWELVE STEPS DOWN. IT MUST BE *JUST* BELOW THE WATER.

TWELVE STEPS DOWN? ARE YOU SURE?

ARE ANY OF THOSE FLASHLIGHTS WATERPROOF?

I DON'T THINK SO. BUT SCOT HAS GLOW STICKS.

WHAT ARE YOU DOING?

I WANT TO SEE IF IT'S THERE. I'LL BE IN AND OUT IN THIRTY SECONDS. KAVANAUGH, GIMME ONE OF THOSE GLOW STICKS.

THAT'S COLD. THAT'S VERY COLD.

THAT'S RIGHT. IT'S COLD LIKE AS IN *HYPOTHERMIA.* AND YOU DON'T KNOW IF THERE'S CURRENTS...

IT'LL BE ALL RIGHT. I'M NOT AFRAID.

I'M NOT QUESTIONING YOUR BRAVERY. I'M QUESTIONING YOUR *INTELLIGENCE.*

KKKK

YEAH. BUT THERE'S SOMETHING I NEED TO SEE RIGHT ON THE OTHER SIDE OF *STUPID*. STAY HERE. I'M GOING TO WANT MY JACKET WHEN I GET OUT.

OH, CAN I STAY HERE? THANKS. THINK I WILL.

HOLYSHIT! HOLYSHIT! HOLYSHIT!

KAVANAUGH! GET DOWN HERE AND SHOW ME WHAT I'M LOOKING FOR!

SPLASH!

COMING, DEAR!

DUDE. WHAT ARE YOU DOING? YOU'RE MAKING A TERRIBLE MISTAKE.

CUTE.

I WON'T DIE FROM A LITTLE COLD.

I'M NOT TALKING ABOUT YOUR LIFE. I'M TALKING ABOUT YOUR TRAGIC CHOICE OF UNDERWEAR AND YOUR DECISION TO LET TWO TOTALLY LIKABLE GIRLS SEE YOU IN THEM.

HOLD THE FORT, JAMAL. IF I DON'T COME BACK, TELL MY MOTHER I LOVED HER.

DON'T WORRY, DUDE. I'M STAYING RIGHT HERE, WHERE I GOT A FRONT ROW SEAT ON WATCHING YOU DROWN.

'SIDES, YOU COULDN'T GET ME DOWN ON THOSE STEPS FOR A FIRST EDITION OF BOSWELL'S *LIFE OF JOHNSON*.

KKKKKKK

DID YOU—

SAW IT! BUT IT'S DOWN, IT'S WAY DOWN, I COULDN'T READ MUCH.

I NEED TO G-GO AGAIN TRY AND GET D-DEEPER

LET ME TRY, I—

ALL RIGHT, KINSEY. YOU *SAW* IT. ENOUGH. COME BACK.

SHE'S NOT HEARING A THING I SAY.

IT'S ALL COOL. THEY'LL BE OUT IN A SEC.

LET'S NOT PANIC UNTIL WE HAVE SOMETHING TO—

EEEEEYAAAAAA!

FUCKING RAT! EVERYONE RUN!

WHAT ARE YOU—

TUMP

crack

40

41

43

YOU REALLY THINK THERE'S ANOTHER P-PLACE WE CAN—

NO.

ME, N-NEITHER. SO WHY ARE WE SWIMMING AROUND? SHOULDN'T WE C-CONSERVE OUR ENERGY?

I W-WUH-WANTED T-TO GET AWAY FROM THEM SO WE C-COULD TALK FOR A M-MINUTE. THEY MIGHT BE RESCUED. BUT—THIS WATER—IT'S SO COLD—I D-DON'T THINK THERE'S MUCH CH-CHANCE...

I KNOW IT. I ALREADY FIGURED THAT OUT. I G-GUESS IF SOMEONE HAS TO BE IN THE WATER, IT OUGHT TO B-BE ME.

IF I DIDN'T FUH-F-FREAK OUT AND JUMP ON THE STAIRS LIKE THAT—I GOT S-SCARED AND PUT US ALL IN THE D-D-DRINK.

I D-DON'T B-B-BELIEVE IT. SS-S-STEPS PROBABLY WOULD'VE FALLEN IN WHEN WE T-TRIED TO CLIMB OUT.

I'M THE ONE WHO FUH-FUH-F-FUCKED UP. I WASN'T S-SCARED *ENOUGH*, MAYBE.

N-NEVER SHOULD'VE GONE OUT ON THE S-STEPS IN THE FIRST P-PUH-PLACE. NEVER SHOULD'VE GONE PAST THE CHAIN-LINK FENCE. I PUH-PUT EVERYONE AT RISK.

YOU WANTED TO KNOW ABOUT YOUR D-DAD. WHO DOESN'T UNDERSTAND THAT?

*

THANKS. STILL. I C-CAN'T HAVE JACKIE DIE C-'CAUSE OF ME.

ANYTHING?

NO.

WHAT ARE WE GOING TO DO?

I DON'T KNOW. JUST WAIT I GUESS. SEE IF ANYONE COMES.

45

COME ON, JAMAL, GRAB MY HANDS SO YOU DON'T HAVE TO PADDLE AROUND TIRING YOURSELF OUT.

KK-K KRAAK

AH!

OKAY, I—

UNH! OW... I... HANG ON...

LUH-LEGGO. NO G-G-GOOD. IF I DON'T PULL THE STRUT DOWN, I'LL YANK YOUR ARMS OUT OF THEIR SUH-S-SOCKETS.

LEAVE IT.

JACKIE. HEY. MY OLDER BROTHER. HIS NAME IS TREAT. DO ME A FAVOR? IF I FREEZE TO DEATH—

STOP RIGHT THERE. THAT'S NOT HAPPENING.

BETTER ASK ME THOSE QUESTIONS, KAVANAUGH. BEFORE I'M. TOO COLD. TO ANSWER 'EM.

KINSEY... I... I DON'T THINK...

...I... THEY WERE JUST STUPID... UNDER THE CIRCUMSTANCES I'D RATHER...

WELL, MAYBE IT IS, MAYBE IT ISN'T. JUST TELL TREAT. ALL MY PORN IS IN A FILE ON MY HARD-DRIVE MARKED SOCIAL STUDIES. I DON'T WANT MOM— YOU KNOW...

YOUR—YOUR— HA-HA-HOKAY. OKAY, JAMAL. IF IT COMES TO THAT.

F-FUCK HIM. I'LL TAKE HIS QUESTIONS IF HE DOESN'T WANT 'EM.

WHAT'S THE BEST THING YOU REMEMBER ABOUT YOUR D-DAD?

HIM READING TO ME. WHEN I WAS LITTLE. WE HAD A B-BLANKET, A SPECIAL READING BLANKET. IT SMELLED LIKE HIM. LIKE—FALL. AUTUMN. FUH-F-FOOTBALL. WHATEVER. LIKE THINGS ENDING.

MY D-DAD AND I BUILT A BARN. FOR HIS BROTHER. IT WAS LIKE THE BEST SUMMER EVER. I'D B-BUILD THAT BARN IN MY SLEEP SOMETIMES, ME AND HIM AND MY OLDER BROTHER.

IS YOUR DAD—?

HE GOT IT IN AFGHANISTAN.

I'M SO. SO. SORRY.

HEY. FEELING IS MUTUAL.

N-NEXT?

WELL, FIRST OF ALL... I LIKE YOU AND EVERYTHING... I MEAN, I DON'T *LIKE* YOU, LIKE YOU, BUT YOU KNOW...

SCOT IS THE ONE WITH THE C-CRUSH AND I IN NO WAY, SHAPE, OR FORM W-WANT TO STEP ON HIS T-TOES...

RIGHT. BROS B-BEFORE HOS. GOT IT. GUH-G-GET TO THE P-POINT BEFORE I DROWN PLEASE.

I'M GOING TO BE SEVENTEEN IN FOUR MONTHS AND MOST GUYS MY AGE HAVE G-GIRLFRIENDS—

BUT DO YOU THINK FOR TEN SECONDS WE COULD BOTH PRETEND—AND YOU COULD—YOU KNOW—

48

ARE YOU ALL RIGHT?

JUST COLD. I'LL LIVE.

NO. I MEAN *MENTALLY.* DO YOU HAVE A DEATH WISH, KINSEY? IS THERE SOMETHING WRONG WITH YOU?

BECAUSE IF THERE IS, I HOPE YOU GET TREATMENT. AND I ALSO HOPE YOU STAY THE FUCK AWAY FROM ME UNTIL YOU GET IT.

COMING DOWN HERE WAS *CRAZY*—AND—AND *DANGEROUS*—AND YOU HAD NO BUSINESS—

—DRAGGING YOU INTO IT. NO. YOU'RE RIGHT. I AGREE.

I'M JUST GLAD YOU'RE OKAY. IF YOU DON'T WANT TO BE MY FRIEND ANYMORE, I UNDERSTAND. CAN'T BLAME YOU.

WILL YOU *STOP* THAT!

WHAT?

BEING SO *FUCKING* REASONABLE. I'M *MAD* AT YOU. CAN'T YOU SEE I'M *MAD* AT YOU? I WAS *SCARED*, KINSEY.

I KNOW. I'M SORRY. I'D RATHER BE DROWNED THAN THINK I GOT SOMEONE KILLED. ESPECIALLY THREE FRIENDS.

TLUC

I'LL KILL YOU.

STOP RUNNING. YOU'RE ONLY MAKING IT WORSE ON YOURSELF.

I'M NOT GIVING YOU YOUR HAT UNTIL I GET THE HEAD KEY BACK!

KEEP IT UP, I'LL OPEN YOUR HEAD THE OLD-FASHIONED WAY. VIA SKULL FRACTURE.

I DON'T EVEN GOT THE FRIGGIN' THING. KINSEY HAS IT. WHY CAN'T YOU PISS HER OFF?

I DON'T KNOW HOW! SHE'S ALWAYS CALM! SHE'S LIKE A POD PERSON. I CAN'T STAND IT!

YEAH. SHE'S MAKING ME NUTS, TOO. LOOK, COME OUT OF THERE, KID, AND I PROMISE YOU WON'T BE HURT.

BEYOND WHAT YOU GOT COMING TO YOU.

NOWHERE LEFT TO GO, IS THERE, YOU LITTLE TURD?

TYLER? TY?

NOWHERE LEFT TO— UNH.

Crown Of
Shadows
CHAPTER THREE:
LAST LIGHT

IT WASN'T MURDER.

OF COURSE IT WASN'T. EVEN IF YOUR SON *HAD* BROKEN SAM LESSER'S NECK—

HE DIDN'T.

—IT WOULD BE AN OBVIOUS CASE OF SELF-DEFENSE.

BUT IT WASN'T SELF-DEFENSE BECAUSE SAM BROKE HIS OWN NECK FALLING DOWN THESE STAIRS, TRYING TO GET AWAY.

I DIDN'T COME HERE TO COLLECT EVIDENCE FOR A CASE AGAINST YOUR SON. *YOU* CALLED *ME*, REMEMBER?

I APOLOGIZE IF IT LOOKS LIKE I'M SNOOPING. YOU DIDN'T ANSWER THE DOOR. I THOUGHT YOU MIGHT BE IN THE BACKYARD.

I'M SORRY. DIDN'T MEAN TO HAUL OUT THE PARANOIA STICK AND BEAT YOU WITH IT.

AFTER WHAT YOU AND YOUR FAMILY HAVE BEEN THROUGH, I'D BE SURPRISED IF YOU WEREN'T ON EDGE.

ESPECIALLY AFTER THE INCIDENT IN CAPE COD LAST FRIDAY NIGHT.

THAT'S WHAT I CALLED ABOUT—THE THING IN PROVINCETOWN.

INTEREST YOU IN A BLOODY MARY?

HM? AH, NO, I DON'T DRINK WHILE I'M THEORETICALLY AT WORK. I WOULDN'T TURN DOWN A CUP OF COFFEE, HOWEVER.

SEE, THAT'S PERFECT. I MADE A POT OUT OF HABIT THIS MORNING, BUT I COULDN'T DRINK ANY. I CAN'T HANDLE CAFFEINE LIKE I USED TO, APPARENTLY. MAKES ME JUMPY. I'M ALREADY TOO JUMPY AS IT IS.

I KEPT WAKING UP THE OTHER NIGHT, THINKING THERE WAS SOMEONE BREAKING INTO THE HOUSE.

I CAN AT LEAST EASE YOUR MIND ON ONE MATTER. WHAT HAPPENED TO BRIAN ROGAN WAS TRAGIC AND A CRIME, BUT IS NOT CONNECTED IN ANY WAY TO WHAT SAM LESSER DID TO YOUR FAMILY.

THE WOMAN WHO RAN HIM DOWN WAS DRUNK, AND HAD EXCHANGED UGLY WORDS WITH MR. ROGAN IN A BAR EARLIER IN THE NIGHT.

IT ISN'T MY AREA, BUT I UNDERSTAND TENSIONS HAVE BEEN HIGH ON THE CAPE IN THE WAKE OF THE RECENT GAY MARRIAGE RULINGS.

ALL RIGHT. AFTER WHAT DUNCAN TOLD ME I DIDN'T THINK THERE WAS ANY CHANCE—BUT HE'S VERY DISTRAUGHT. I FIGURED I'D BETTER GET A SECOND OPINION.

I UNDERSTAND. I'M GLAD TO BE YOUR SOUNDING BOARD, MRS. LOCKE.

ARE YOU?

IS THERE SOMETHING MORE?

REMEMBER HOW SAM WAS FIXATED ON FINDING A COUPLE OF OLD KEYS?

I CAME ACROSS SOMETHING THE OTHER NIGHT. FOUND IT JUST A FEW FEET FROM WHERE SAM DIED, ACTUALLY, IN THAT LITTLE PARLOR. NO IDEA HOW IT GOT THERE. MAYBE THAT'S WHY IT'S BOTHERING ME... THE WAY IT JUST SHOWED UP OUT OF NOWHERE.

HOW CURIOUS.

ISN'T IT? SAM SAID ONE OF THE KEYS HE WAS LOOKING FOR HAD RINGS CONNECTED TO RINGS. *THIS* HAS RINGS CONNECTED TO RINGS.

SAM LESSER HAD HOMEMADE TATTOOS SHOWING KEYS OF DIFFERENT SORTS. I WONDER IF THIS MATCHES ANY OF THEM. I COULD COMPARE TO THE PHOTO RECORD. NOT THAT IT MATTERS, BUT... IT'S INTERESTING.

THANKS FOR LISTENING TO MY CRAZY TALK.

MRS. LOCKE, LAST YEAR A DERANGED MAN ASSAULTED ME WITH A DEATH RAY MADE OUT OF A TOILET PLUNGER AND TINFOIL. I GREW UP IN A NATION WHERE CHILDREN CARRY MACHINE GUNS.

MY MOTHER ENROLLED ME IN FENCING CLASSES AFTER SHE HAD A DREAM THAT SOMEDAY I WOULD NEED TO DEFEND MYSELF WITH A SWORD.

I WOULDN'T KNOW CRAZY IF IT BIT ME IN THE FACE.

HM. I WONDER—

CLINK CLINK

FINISHED LOOKING THROUGH MY THINGS?

I WAS TRYING TO FIND THE CHARGER FOR YOUR—

I'VE GOT A TRAVEL CHARGER IN THE CAR. I THINK YOU KNOW THAT.

I TURNED A BLIND EYE TO YOU TIPTOEING INTO THE HOUSE THE OTHER DAY AFTER YOU WENT FOR A SWIM WITH THOSE BOYS TILL ALMOST DARK. I CAN FORGIVE YOU BEING A LITTLE WILD. BUT NOT BEING A SNEAK.

THAT'S FUNNY, MOM. I CAN FORGIVE *YOU* FOR BEING SUSPICIOUS AND MEAN AND ANGRY ALL THE TIME—AFTER WHAT YOU WENT THROUGH IN WILLITS, YOU'VE EARNED IT—

YOU DON'T KNOW ANYTHING ABOUT IT.

—BUT I HAVE A HARDER TIME FORGIVING YOU FOR BEING A SHITTY, IRRESPONSIBLE DRUNK. WAKING TYLER UP IN THE MIDDLE OF THE NIGHT TO CRY ALL OVER HIM. LIKE HE ISN'T DEALING WITH A FEW THINGS HIMSELF.

YOU MOUTHY LITTLE... I OUGHTA—

CHRIST. YOU'VE ALREADY BEEN DRINKING. I CAN SMELL IT ON YOUR BREATH. AT LEAST YOU'RE ONLY DRIVING *YOURSELF.* I CAN'T IMAGINE YOU TAKING BODE IN THE CAR.

GO FOR A WALK, KINSEY.

OR WHAT? YOU GOING TO DRAG ME OUT? IT'S MY HOUSE TOO, TYLER, AND YOU CAN'T SCARE ME INTO—

I KNOW I CAN'T. THAT'S WHY I'M ASKING. PLEASE. BE DONE HERE.

I DON'T EVEN KNOW WHO YOU ARE ANYMORE, KINSEY.

YOU GOT THAT RIGHT. YOU DON'T KNOW.

YOU CRASH THE CAR DRIVING DRUNK, I'M NOT GOING TO CRY OVER IT. I'M ALL CRIED OUT THESE DAYS AND YOU KNOW WHAT YOU'RE DOING. IN THEORY.

CHRIST. WILL YOU. GET. OUT?

MOM. SHE DIDN'T MEAN—

SHE MEANT EVERY WORD.

YOU KNOW... WE'VE TALKED ABOUT WHAT HAPPENED TO DAD IN WILLITS BUT WE... WE NEVER TALK ABOUT WHAT HAPPENED TO...

WILL YOU LEAVE ME ALONE, TYLER? I NEED A SECOND.

TELL YOUR MOTHER A DASTARDLY LIE AND COME AWAY WITH US. DON'T ASK QUESTIONS. WE'RE NOT GOING TO TELL YOU WHERE WE'RE GOING ANYWAY. JUST COME ALONG.

AH, GUYS. I CAN'T. NOT TONIGHT. SORRY.

AREN'T YOU AT LEAST A LITTLE CURIOUS ABOUT OUR LATEST DEATH-DEFYING DESTINATION?

NO. NOT REALLY. IT DOESN'T MATTER.

DAMN, WOMAN. YOU'RE RELENTLESS. ALL RIGHT, I'LL TELL.

WE'RE OFF TO BOSTON TO SEE MUSE AT THE BEACON FOR A NIGHT OF PERSONAL TRANSCENDENCE THROUGH LOUD, ARTY ENGLISH PROG ROCK. YOU SURE YOU CAN'T NIP OFF WITH US?

61

YOU'VE GOT A RIDE INTO BOSTON?

AH, NOT YET.

DID YOU CHECK TO SEE IF IT'S AN ALL-AGES SHOW?

ACTUALLY, IT'S 21 AND OLDER.

SO YOU'VE GOT FAKE IDS?

ER, NO.

SO, YOU'VE GOT NO RIDE—AND NO WAY TO GET IN—AND NO MONEY.

BOY, THIS SOUNDS LIKE A HELLUVA NIGHT.

YOUR SARCASM NEVER FAILS TO GIVE ME A DELICIOUS LITTLE THRILL.

WHO'S BEING SARCASTIC? I WISH I COULD GO WITH YOU GUYS. I REALLY DO. *BUT.* I'M ON KID DUTY WITH TY. SORRY.

ENH, DON'T WORRY ABOUT IT. I DON'T THINK WE'RE ACTUALLY GOING ANYWHERE.

IT'S A NICE DAYDREAM BUT 20-TO-1 SAYS WE DON'T GET ANY FURTHER THAN THE COMIC SHOP IN DOWNTOWN LOVECRAFT.

OH, HEY. WE KIND OF... GOT YOU A GIFT. WE BOTH CHIPPED IN ON IT.

WHAT'S THIS?

A CUTE LITTLE SOMETHING. TOKEN OF GRATITUDE. FOR SAVING OUR LIVES.

SOMETHING TO WEAR?

MMHM.

OKAY—WAIT. WHAT IS IT?

PRACTICAL. IT'S PRACTICAL.

BUT HOT.

BE DELIGHTED TO SEE YOU IN IT, LUV. BIT REVEALING, THOUGH. BIT KINKY. NOT THE KIND OF THING I THINK YOU'D HAVE THE NERVE TO WEAR TO SCHOOL.

IF I DIDN'T KNOW BETTER I'D THINK THAT WAS A DARE.

HEY, MOM. NOTHING, JUST SITTING HERE SWEATING OVER MY HOMEWORK. HOW'S DUNK?

I MADE HIM GO HOME AND GET SOME SLEEP. HE'S BARELY LEFT THE HOSPITAL IN DAYS.

LISTEN, I'M GOING TO GET BACK LATER THAN I THOUGHT. I OVERSTAYED AT DUNCAN'S AND MISSED THE LAST FERRY BY TEN MINUTES. I'M GOING TO HAVE TO DRIVE THE LONG WAY. I'M... IN THE CAR NOW.

WHAT? NO, MOM, DON'T DO THAT. YOU SOUND WIPED AND IT'S LIKE NINE ALREADY. IT'S TOO FAR TO DRIVE THIS LATE.

JUST STAY AT DUNCAN'S. WE'RE FINE. NOTHING IS GOING TO HAPPEN.

WAIT. *WAIT*. WHO'S COMING BY? YOU DON'T NEED ANYONE TO CHECK ON US.

HE'S *NOT* CHECKING UP ON YOU. HE JUST WANTS TO DROP SOMETHING OFF.

...

OKAY. SO I CALLED AND ASKED IF HE'D SWING BY. FOR A MINUTE. DON'T BE MAD, TYLER. I TRUST YOU. I'M JUST... NOT THERE.

UN-HUH. OKAY. WHEN DOES HE GET OFF WORK?

NO. THAT'S FINE. I'LL STILL BE UP.

MOM. YOU DON'T HAVE TO APOLOGIZE. I UNDERSTAND. I AM MR. UNDERSTANDING.

LOVE TO DUNCAN. LOVE YOU.

SEE YOU TOMORROW MORNING.

WHERE'D YOU PUT IT, RENDELL?

NO. TOO OBVIOUS.

ONE OF THESE LOOSE?

WAKE ALL THE SHADOWS IN THE HOUSE.

I NEED YOU TO LOOK EVERYWHERE. FIND THE KEY TO THE WELLHOUSE...

...AND THE KEY TO THE BLACK DOOR.

DON'T WORRY. I'LL BE HELPING YOU LOOK. BUT FIRST I PROBABLY OUGHT TO SLIP INTO SOMETHING MORE COMFORTABLE.

UHH...
...NOOO... I DON'T THINK SO. PROBABLY OUGHT TO BE SOMETHING A BIT MORE BADASS...

HM. A LITTLE TOO NINJA.
BESIDES. I NEED A LOOK THAT'LL THROW THEM OFF. AND REALLY, THEY'RE EXPECTING...

...BODE'S DARK LADY FROM THE WELL.

- Pic. 04 -

thump

(9:23) **JSAT:** Got to go dudes.
Got a hot date with my right hand.
Night Scot. Night, K.
Stay dry.

(9:23) **HOLEINTHEHEADK:** LOL. TMI.
Stay dry.

(9:24) **DEVILWSHPR13:** Stay dry, mates.

03. OUT OF MYSELF

THE FUCK?

AA!

73

Crown Of Shadows
CHAPTER FOUR: SHADOW PLAY

UR. WHO SHIT IN MY MOUTH?

UNNH. YOU HER? THE DARK GIRL BODE MET IN THE WELLHOUSE?

THE ONE WHO SENT SAM LESSER TO KILL MY DAD?

YEAH, I WAS HOPING I'D GET A CHANCE TO SAY HELLO TO YOU SOMETIME.

PTTH.

HOW DO YOU DO?

TYLER?
BODE?

KIN—
SSSEEEEY!

PLEASE...

...PLEASE...

UH, IT'S A LITTLE HARD— UPSIDE-DOWN...

UGHUGHUGH!

KEYS
KEYS, OKAY!
GOTYA!

THE OMEGA
KEY. I KNOW
ABOUT THAT
ONE. WHAT'S
THE OTHER?

THE
WELLHOUSE?

YOU WANT
A KEY TO THE
WELLHOUSE? WHY?
YOU'RE ALREADY
FREE.

UNLESS
SOMEONE WITH
THAT KEY COULD
MAKE YOU GO AWAY.
THAT IT?

AND WHY THE
FUCK DON'T YOU
SAY ANYTHING?
CAN'T YOU TALK?
YOU TALKED TO
BODE.

MOM. YOU THINK MY MOM HAS IT.

HUH. ALL RIGHT. I GUESS THERE'S NO POINT TRYING TO LIE. YOU'RE HALF-RIGHT. I MEAN, SHE *DID* HAVE IT.

BUT SHE GAVE IT TO ME AND TOLD ME TO PUT IT IN A SAFE PLACE.

SO I STUCK IT UP MY ASS. YOU WANT IT BACK, YOU'LL HAVE TO REACH ON UP THERE AND GET IT.

FFFFFUH— UCK!

MOTHER *FUCKER!*

I CAN'T WAIT TO CLIMB DOWN FROM HERE AND GET LARGE ON YOU, BITCH.

KINNSEEEEY!

OPEN THE DOOR!

UNH—BODEEE! OH—MMM—PEN THE FUH—ERNN—KING

I'M TRYING I'M *TRYING*...

ARE YOU ALL RIGHT?

I'M SCARED.

HEY, WHO WOULDN'T BE?

YOU. WHAT ARE THEY?

I THINK THEY'RE JUST—SHADOWS. COME TO LIFE SOMEHOW.

"HOW'D YOU WIND UP IN THE KITCHEN, BODE?"

"MY SHADOW HAD ME ALL WRAPPED UP IN THIS STUFF, BUT HE LEFT A HAND FREE."

"SO WHEN HE WAS DRAGGING ME THROUGH THE KITCHEN, I GRABBED THE FRIDGE DOOR..."

"ONE OF THEM GRABBED ME AND DRAGGED ME DOWNSTAIRS. I DON'T KNOW WHERE HE WAS TRYING TO TAKE ME.

"THERE WERE LOTS OF OTHER SHADOWS, TOO. LOOKING THROUGH MY DRESSER AND STUFF."

"...AND YANKED MYSELF FREE. IT WAS WEIRD. HE JUST GAVE UP. I DON'T THINK HE REALLY WANTED TO TAKE ME PRISONER.

"I TURNED ON THE LIGHTS AND BLOCKED THE DOORS AND I'VE BEEN HERE EVER SINCE."

DID YOU TRY CALLING—

THEY SMASHED THE PHONE.

YEAH. OKAY. YOU DID GOOD, BODE.

ARE WE GOING TO BE ALL RIGHT?

ARE YOU KIDDING? THESE GUYS ARE PUSHOVERS. THEY'RE LIKE MOST MONSTERS... ONLY SCARY IN THE DARK. YOU TURN ON THE LIGHTS AND THEY MELT AWAY. THAT'S WHAT'S KEEPING THEM OUT. IT ISN'T THE STUFF AGAINST THE DOOR. IT'S THE LIGHT.

THAT'S WHY YOUR SHADOW LET YOU GO, TOO, I BET. THE LIGHT FROM THE FRIDGE. DAMN, I SHOULD'VE BEEN SWITCHING ON LIGHTS AS I CAME THIS WAY. STUPID.

WELL. WHAT IF THEY—

HE'S DRIVING AWAY!

GODDAMNIT, OPEN THE WINDOW!

I CAN'T, THE LOCK'S ARE STUCK, CAN YOU—

SKKSH!

...AND IT'S A GOOD ONE FOR THE HALLOWEEN SEASON, IT'S CALLED "COMPLICATED SHADOWS," CHECK IT OUT...

HE'S GONE!

OH, BOY.

C'MON!

WHERE IS IT? WHERE'S THE WELLHOUSE KEY?

WHAT? *WHO?* KINSEY?

HOW COULD SHE TAKE IT AWAY FROM YOU? DOES SHE HAVE SOME KIND OF LIGHT? FLASHLIGHT OR SOMETHING?

I DON'T CARE WHAT SHE HAS. MAKE ENOUGH DARKNESS AND HER DIM LITTLE LIGHT WON'T MEAN A FUCKING THING.

ALL SHADOWS TO ME!

Crown Of Shadows
CHAPTER FIVE: LIGHT OF DAY

UHKK ...
GUUUH...

EVIDENCE C-172

IT'S OKAY, KID.

I THINK IT'S OVER.

SEE. THERE'S YOUR BIG BRO.

NO PUN INTENDED.

YOU GUYS ALL RIGHT?

YEAH. YOU?

FINE. HERE, CLIMB UP. I WANT TO SHOW YOU SOMETHING.

GOD. I THINK THESE ARE MINE.

TYLER?

WHEN I WALKED IN THIS HOUSE I THOUGHT I WAS GOING TO FIND YOU DEAD.

IN A FEW MINUTES, YOU'RE GOING TO WISH I DID.

UHH... YEAH. ME AND KINSEY KIND OF HAD SOME FRIENDS OVER AND SHIT GOT A LITTLE OUT OF HAND...

BUT I WILL *TOTALLY* CLEAN UP. AND... PAY FOR THE BROKEN WINDOWS.

WINDOWS? PLURAL?

NICE ONE, HIDING OUT HERE. I THOUGHT YOU WEREN'T AFRAID OF ANYTHING.

IT'S NOT A QUESTION OF FEAR. STAYING OUT OF HER WAY THIS MORNING IS JUST GOOD SENSE.

HOW'D SHE—

BETTER THAN I THOUGHT. SHE DIDN'T SAY MUCH.

THAT'S 'CAUSE SHE'S ASHAMED.

SHE'S—THE FUCK YOU TALKING ABOUT?

MISSED THE FERRY. SURE SHE DID.

KINSEY? WHERE YOU GOING, GIRL? WE EXPECTING A FLOOD?

NO, REALLY. WHAT'S UP WITH THE LIFE PRESERVER?

SOME FRIENDS GAVE IT TO ME. SO I'M WEARING IT.

UHH... YEAH. OKAY. SERIOUSLY. DO YOU HAVE ANY IDEA HOW... LAME YOU LOOK... I MEAN, THERE ARE PEOPLE LAUGHING...

MY FRIENDS WILL THINK IT'S COOL. I'M NOT REALLY WORRIED ABOUT ANYONE ELSE'S OPINION.

HEY! JAMAL! SCOT!

WAIT. THOSE ARE THE FRIENDS WE'RE TALKING ABOUT? KAVANAUGH AND SATURDAY? HEY, I HAVEN'T BEEN AT LOVECRAFT ACADEMY ANY LONGER THAN YOU, BUT EVEN I KNOW THAT HANGING OUT WITH THOSE TWO IS JUMPING OFF THE SOCIAL CLIFF INTO THE DEEP SEAS OF UNCOOL...

THAT SO? WELL I GUESS THIS IS WHERE I SAY "GERONIMO."

WHATEVER. WE'LL TALK ABOUT THIS AT LUNCH.

I'LL BE SITTING WITH THEM AT LUNCH. SO IF YOU WANT TO BE WITH ME, GUESS YOU'LL HAVE TO JUMP, TOO.

HEY, GUYS! WAIT UP!

TYLER! TYLER LOCKE!

WHAT'S UP? JORDAN?

WHAT THE FUCK IS THIS?

AN "F"? A FUCKING "F"? CHRIST, WHAT KIND OF *RETARD* ARE YOU? I DIDN'T EVEN DO THE READING, AND I COULD'VE FAKED MY WAY TO A "*D*."

SHE FLUNKED IT? MRS. CORNWELL FLUNKED YOUR PAPER? WHY? DID SHE SAY—

"SHOWS NO COMPREHENSION OF THE CORE IDEAS," SHE SAID. "PLOT SUMMARIES ARE NOT THE SAME AS UNDERSTANDING," SHE SAID.

I TRUSTED YOU AND YOU *FUCKED* ME, LOCKE!

AGGH! EVERY TIME I START TO PITY YOU A LITTLE, YOU TURN INTO A *FUCKING* FREAK ON ME!

JUST STAY THE *FUCK* AWAY FROM ME, BEFORE YOU COMPLETELY RUIN MY LIFE!

M-MOM?

I F-FELL DOWN AND HURT MYSELF.

OH, KIDDO.

WHAT ARE YOU WATCHING?

AH—JUST AN OLD VIDEOTAPE. MRS. MAYHEW IN WILLITS FOUND IT AND—

IT'S DAD.

LET'S TRY THIS AGAIN. KNOCK-KNOCK.

WHO'S THERE?

WHO'S THERE?

WANDA

WANDA WHO?

WANDA SEE ME JUGGLE? I'M REALLY GOOD AT IT.

HE'S JUGGLING.

YEAH. THE BIG OL' SHOWOFF.

ALL BETTER. NOTHING BROKE MOM DOESN'T KNOW HOW TO FIX.

DARE I ASK HOW YOU GOT YOURSELF BLOODIED UP?

WHAT IN THE NAME OF THOMAS H. CRAPPER—?

WHAT EXACTLY WERE YOU TRYING TO ACCOMPLISH?

"I SAW SOMETHING UP THERE."

AND YOU WERE TRYING TO GET IT WITH THIS? THIS IS MY OLD CANE, ISN'T IT?

IT WAS ALREADY BROKEN.

I KNOW.

LET'S SEE. WHAT DO WE HAVE HERE?

A KEY. ANOTHER GODDAMN... OKAY. WELL. ONE MORE FOR THE COLLECTION.

I WONDER WHAT IT DOES?

WHAT IT DOES? IT OPENS THIS MEDICINE CABINET. THAT'S WHAT IT DOES.

DOESN'T MAKE YOU INTO A GHOST. DOESN'T OPEN YOUR HEAD.

WHAT IT DOES IS MAGICALLY GIVE US A PLACE TO STICK SOME BROKEN SHIT.

END OF STORY.

CLICK!

BLAAACH

HEY, BUDDY. YOU WANNA NOT SPLAT ALL OF THOSE? SOME OF US LIKE THOSE FOR BREAKFAST.

SORR-EE!

MM. WHAT DID THE GRAPEFRUITS DO TO YOU, ANYWAY?

I'M TRYIN' TO JUGGLE! LIKE DAD USETA.

TELL YOU WHAT, KID. I CAN'T DO IT LIKE YOUR FATHER COULD— HE COULD GET FOUR OR FIVE THINGS IN THE AIR AT ONCE.

BUT I DO HAVE A HANDLE ON THE BASIC TECHNIQUE.

IT'S LIKE—WHILE ONE IS IN THE AIR—

—SEE, YOU PASS WITH YOUR OTHER HAND—

KRAAAK PASSSHH

SHIT. WELL. AT LEAST THEY WERE THE UGLY DISHES.

NOW THAT JUST BOTHERS ME.

HEY, BUD, I'LL READ TO YOU. WANNA GO HAVE SOME *BONEVILLE*?

OKAY.

GO GET IN YOUR JAMMIES THEN. I'LL BE RIGHT UP.

MOM. IF SOMETHING'S WRONG—

YOUR DAD GOT SHOT IN THE FACE THIS SUMMER AND I HAVE APPARENTLY FORGOTTEN HOW TO JUGGLE.

THAT'S WHAT'S WRONG.

AH... ARE YOU GOING TO BE OKAY IF I TAKE OFF? I TOLD ZACK I'D STUDY WITH HIM AT HIS PLACE. I'LL BE BACK BY ELEVEN.

I'M FINE, TY. A LITTLE OVERTIRED. GO ON. DON'T BE BACK TOO LATE.

HE'S SO *WEIRD*, JACKIE. HE SAW ME MESSAGING ON MY CELL PHONE AND IT WAS LIKE HE HAD NEVER SEEN A TEXT BEFORE.

I GUESS ZACK'S PARENTS ARE SUPER BACK-TO-NATURE HIPPIE TYPES OR SOMETHING. LIKE THEY'D GIVE HIM SEEDS FOR CHRISTMAS AND STUFF.

TOMATO SEEDS! I DON'T THINK THEY'RE THAT WILD...

125

LET'S SEE WHAT YOU CAN DO WITH...

...AA! *KE*-RIST.

OH, *I* GET IT NOW. THAT'S PART OF IT. YOU CAN CHANGE SHAPE TO FIX WHATEVER NEEDS FIXING.

NICE.

HUNH? BODE?

EVERYBODY. STOP. FIGHTING.

BODE... DON'T. JUST DON'T. I'LL PUT HIM BACK IN BED.

MOVE OUT OF MY WAY OR—

OR WHAT? DON'T YOU GET IT? YOU'VE GOT NOTHING TO THREATEN ME WITH.

I'LL TAKE CARE OF HIM. YOU'RE NOT UP TO IT TONIGHT. OR MOST NIGHTS.

SAY IT.

I CAN'T BELIEVE YOU'D USE YOUR HANDS ON HER. AFTER THE SHIT THIS FAMILY HAS BEEN THROUGH. AFTER SAM LESSER BEAT HER UNCONSCIOUS.

AS FOR THE REST OF YOUR SHIT—YOUR MOODS, YOUR DRINKING—I CAN TAKE WHATEVER YOU CAN DISH OUT. SO CAN KINSEY.

BUT IF YOU EVER PUT BODE THROUGH THE EMOTIONAL WRINGER LIKE THIS AGAIN, SO HELP ME—

SHIT. LOOK AT THIS PLACE.

I'LL GET THE BATHROOM.

HEY, TY. HOW'S IT GOING? NEED ANY HELP IN THERE?

TY?

ΩMeGa KeY

...in our ... & I resolve'd ... hazzarded such a look ... song I work'd in a fever ... till finallie t'was cast ... oh how I feer'd! My ... in the gath'r'd ... straiked ou... held the do... beig'd ... Gonn... ho...

THE KNOWN KEYS
(EXCERPTS FROM THE DIARY OF
BENJAMIN PIERCE LOCKE, 1757 - 1799)

GHoST KeY

onlee in occaisonull daith do I find peece now, for with the bode caste aisyde, it is possibull for one to know his own ETERNAIL SOULE. My spairt cannot leeve the grounds of Keyhowse, but heyre I walke laik an aingel! I aim everywhare and nowhare at once, from the tall's towair, to the deepst caves. It is hard to dreem thair could be any dore more terryble or wondairfulle than that wych dyvydes deth from lyfe, yet my expairances at the thraishold of the black dore have teach'd me thair are worse things than to dyye...

eCHo KeY

whence I unlock'd the dore I heerd a voice that saimed to ecka from the well & it aisk'd me who I sot & I spake of my brother: No sooner had the words pass'd my lips thence he ROSE from the WELL like a spairt & yet was living flaish, alltho he had dyed in the Drowning Caves not 6 weeks beefor. He clasp'd me to his bosom & sayd why do ye look so unhappy to see me brother, but I wast in feer for my allmaighty SOUL & fled to the howse & pray'd thair to the LORD
But in that grait howse, an ecko of my voice was all the reeply I receiv'd

aNYWHeRe KeY

us'd the key to anyplaice againe, to return to Boston, & gaither intelaigents for Crais. Tis an act of terryble wychcraift, but better I do it, than my sister, who is obssaissed with REVENGING herself upon the RED-COATS, for thair violence agin our faither & brother & belov'd maither. Aye, my dredd of beeing called to acconnt someday by SATAN HIMSELF is a trifling concern when maiched with my desyre to rid the worlde of the devylls who taik the King's Coyne to do raip & murdur...

HeaD KeY

of alle the keys I have forged from the WHISP'RING IRON, 'tis the key that opens the human mind I most regrait. Miranda hast a pervairse fasinaytion whist the key & hast us'd ait to fill her head with all thair is to know about WAR & the SLAIYING of MEN, & she carrys an arsanall whist her whairever she goes. Yet I am less in dred of what she has put in than what she hast remov'd. Sometimes it is as if she is now without FEER and indeed is herself more man than I!

GeNDeR KeY

my sister - or should I now say my brother! - fights the shadow war with Crais in the streets of Boston whilst I wait at home, like a helpless maiden, praying to the ALLMAIGHTY! for her safe return. When first I fashin'd the key, I imagined she maight trainsform to a boy to protect her, if necessaire, from the unsavorie lusts of ENGLISHMEN should the King's foot-soldiers return to Lovecraft to abuse God fairing womain. Never did I think she wouldst WILLENGLY caist off the wardrobe of her femininitie for this ruggaid liberation among men...

SHaDoW KeY

O Wycked Night! Damn'd be Crais &
Damn'd be the Redcoats & Damn'd
be my own foole self. Miranda 'tis
griev'sly hurt & lingers on the
thraishold of deth! The Redcoats pursued
her & the tattr'd reminante of Crais's
companie into the caves but I drove
them back with the aide of the lyving
shadows. If she dies I wouldst rather
be a shadow myself than remain in
thys diabollicall world, knowing she
wouldst never have been at riske if
not for me!

GiaNT KeY

she is dying & thair is nothing I can
do to save her!
The Redcoats return'd to assalle the
house & claym her & I admitte I
lette my fury & miserie get the
better of me. I used the giant's
key to multiplie my syze, so that
my body was as vaste as my hayte
& I turn'd upon a wholle regiment
& ~ O GOD forgive me! ~ did
detestably murther them alle!

MeNDiNG KeY

the Iron whispr'd to me laste night
& I work'd in a fever alle day, mayking
a cabinet & forging a new key out of
that dreadfull metal that is not metal.
Yet if the devil may pervairt Holie
'Scripture to serve his purposes, so may
the rihteous at times turn the DEVYLLS
TOOLS to do the work of SWEET JESU!
For the key & cabinet I fashin'd could
be used to mend fraicturd objykts ~
shatter'd plattes, crack'd eggs & broken
sistairs. Bless'd be THE LORD, Miranda
hast recovr'd! I only wish she wouldst
remembair her place & become the
demure & modestte girlle she once was,
but fear her love for Crais will emperille
her againe soon enough...

WELLHOUSE CROSS SECTION